God's Word on Sex and Dating

by

Susan Nemeth

iUniverse, Inc.
New York   Bloomington

God's Word on Sex and Dating

iUniverse books may be ordered through booksellers or by contacting:

iUniverse
1663 Liberty Drive
Bloomington, IN 47403
www.iuniverse.com
1-800-Authors (1-800-288-4677)

Because of the dynamic nature of the Internet, any Web addresses or links contained in this book may have changed since publication and may no longer be valid. The views expressed in this work are solely those of the author and do not necessarily reflect the views of the publisher, and the publisher hereby disclaims any responsibility for them.

ISBN: 978-1-4401-7432-2 (pbk)
ISBN: 978-1-4401-7433-9 (cloth)
ISBN: 978-1-4401-7434-6 (ebook)

Printed in the United States of America

iUniverse rev. date: 10/28/09

First of all, I want to thank God for the awesome family I was raised in and the strength He gave me to live a godly life and to stay pure for my husband. I thank my husband, Frank, for always believing in me and encouraging me to do things I never thought I could. He was my biggest supporter while I wrote this. Also, I thank my children (Jennifer, Frank Jr., and Dave) and my daughters-in-law (both named Angela) for pushing me forward in my work and for being the wonderful young adults that they are. I thank my sister, Dr. Joyce Eckard, for her input and help on the sexually transmitted diseases chapter. Thanks guys ... I couldn't have written this book without all of you.

Contents

Introduction

As long as I can remember, I have loved God. I grew up in a Christian family that not only talked about God, but actually lived in a godly manner. I thank my mom and dad for that. I didn't realize it at the time, but I had what some would call "the perfect childhood." We had our share of problems, but there was always peace and laughter in our home. I had so much fun as a teenager. I guess I didn't realize it until I was older, but those years were fun because I put God first and hung out with friends who loved God too. There was no pressure to do wrong things or go to inappropriate places. We just had fun. When I started dating, I determined in my heart that I would date only Christian guys. That didn't stop temptation, but it sure helped a lot. My goal was to stay pure sexually for my husband. That, to me, was the greatest gift I could give him on our wedding night. It wasn't that my parents drilled that into me, but I just loved God so much that I knew I wanted to please Him.

I graduated from Zion Bible College, got married, and ended up in full-time ministry. My husband, Frank, was a youth pastor. We worked together with youth for almost twenty years and have now pastored a church for the past fifteen years. During those years, we have seen some of our youth give in to the pressures of sex. We sat with some of those girls as they told their parents they were pregnant. We cried with the parents because we knew the heartache that was ahead. We knew that sex was God's gift to marriage and that the church should be the place to hear it taught in the right way. We started teaching a lot of what is in this book. We have a passion to show young people that they *can* stay pure until marriage. We want them to know that they can have happy, fun-filled dates and still stay pure.

I want you young people who are reading this book, whether you are twelve years old or thirty years old, to stay pure for your own sake. Marriage is wonderful, but if you enter it with "baggage" you will have to work even harder. If you have already messed up in the sex area, don't stop reading. God will forgive you when you ask, and you can start new from here. Did you even know that God talked so much about sex? Read on ...

Chapter 1—All about Sex

You're pregnant! The test is positive. What do you do now? You have to tell your boyfriend. When and how do you tell your parents? You wonder how you let yourself get to this point. How will you reach your goals now? Is abortion really wrong?

I wrote this book to give you more knowledge about sex and dating so the scene you just read won't happen to you. We hear about sex every day, but not many people actually look at the behind-the-scenes events that happen. As you read, I hope you will see sex and dating in a new way. It is a wonderful part of life if done right. I don't want to force my religious views on anyone, but the contents of this book include a lot about the Bible. It is your choice to believe it or reject it. I just know that it works.

What Is Sex?

Sex is not just a man and woman coming together physically; it can and should be so much more. The greatest sexual relationship comes from communication, understanding, and trust. In the Bible, the words used for sexual intercourse are "to know." A husband and wife need to know each other in the deepest part of their emotions. Good sex begins in your head, not in the bed.

Sex is one of God's good gifts. God thought it up, but, like many other of God's good gifts, man has distorted it today. Sex can be compared to fire. It is warm and wonderful on a cold night in a fireplace, but that same fire can also burn your house down.

Most people think of sexual intercourse as a physical commitment, but it is also an emotional and spiritual commitment that two people make to each other. If you have the physical without the spiritual part (which is marriage), two things can happen: You will either feel guilty and have low self-esteem, or you will become hardened to your emotions and the spiritual tug in your life. Both results lead to unhappiness.

Sex is meant to bond a married couple together so they become one flesh. It is more than physical. It is an expression of a commitment made for a lifetime. Married couples spend more time talking, solving problems, and doing practical things than having sex. Dating is not a lifetime commitment, so sex should not be part of dating.

"While sex is an expression of love, love is much more than sex; while sex should be fun, it is not a toy; and while one's sexual feelings are very important in the development of personality, sex is not the most important thing in life." 1

The Bible and Sex

The Bible is a very sexual book. It speaks about sex without embarrassment or shame. It openly shows the sexual sins of people. You can read about Lot's daughters having sex with him in Genesis 19:30–38, or David's adultery with Bathsheba in II Samuel, Chapter 11. These are just a couple of the many examples in the Bible.

Have you ever received a love letter? Do you remember how romantic it was to you? The Song of Solomon in the Bible is a drama of two lovers. The way it is worded might sound funny to us today, but it is the correspondence between two people madly in love. God is just reminding us that romance was His idea in the first place. It begins with "Kiss me with the kisses of your mouth, because your love is better than wine" (Song of Solomon 1:2). "My darling, you are like a mare among the king's stallions" (Song of Solomon 1:9). "My lover's left hand is under my head, and his right arm holds me tight." (Song of Solomon 2:6). "My bride, your lips drip honey; honey and milk are under your tongue" (Song of Solomon 4:9). You get the picture, right? (These scriptures are taken from the New Century Version Bible.)

The Bible teaches us that sexual actions have consequences. The tragedy of David and Bathsheba is only one example. (See II Samuel, Chapter 11). Bathsheba was the beautiful woman, Uriah was her husband and one of David's generals in his army, and David was the king. David lusted after Bathsheba and sent for her. They acted on impulse, had an affair, and Bathsheba became pregnant. David then sent Uriah to the front lines of battle where the chances were high that he would be killed. Here began a history of tragedy. Later David repented, but history could not be changed, and scars could not be erased. And, even though God forgave him, David reaped the consequences of his actions for the rest of his life.

The Bible is not a manual on the techniques of sex. It is a guide to the *values* of sex and the *proper perspective* of sex.

Chapter 2—Christ and Sex

Don't be afraid to give your sex life over to Christ. When you do, you will find that He gives you a new way to look at it. Sex, like everything else surrendered to Christ, will have new meaning. Don't pretend that sexual desires don't exist, but learn to make other traits more important in your life. When you focus on honesty, loyalty, self-control, being kind, and having respect for others, the need to please yourself will diminish. Abstinence is something you will want to do so you can develop these other, more important qualities. People will naturally be attracted to you because of your inner beauty.

Your spiritual, mental, and physical lives all work together. Each one affects the others. You are made up of spirit, soul, and body. If you sin with your body, your spiritual walk will be damaged. As a Christian, you have the promise that Jesus will help you resist temptation (I Corinthians 10:13). You can "walk in the Spirit" and not feel forced to give into the desires of your human nature.

With God's help you can have freedom ...

- from outward peer pressure to have premarital sex.
- from inward obsession for premarital sex.
- from a fear of the unknown about sex.
- to be comfortable spending time with the opposite sex.
- to save sex for marriage
- to accept God's forgiveness if you have already blown it.

Biblical freedom is not the ability to do whatever we want, but the power to do what is right. We have freedom in Christ, but not an "anything goes" type of freedom. No one has that freedom; every group has patterns and rules. True freedom is an honest and open acceptance of sexuality and the freedom to talk about it. Hundreds of years ago, sex was a private thing and no one talked about it, especially in church. Young people knew it was wrong outside of marriage, but no one ever said why it was wrong. Today we can talk about it openly.

The World's View of Sex

The world says that anything goes. They do away with rules such as the Ten Commandments. ("Thou shalt not commit adultery" Exodus 20:14.) The world lacks an important part in its belief. With all of its emphasis on the worth of persons (putting the individual person first), they seem to crowd God out of the picture. "Love your neighbor as yourself" is the second great commandment (Matthew 22:39). To love God with your entire being; heart, soul, strength, and mind must take first place. (See Matthew 22:36–38.)

The world falls apart in its idea of love. It fails to distinguish between shallow love that says, "I love sex and want you" (as a sexual partner), and true, romantic love that wants to honor the one loved and says, "You are the only one for me." When you really love a person, you will not want to use that person to satisfy your own desires. Instead, you will want to commit yourself to your lover. That commitment is the foundation of marriage. Real love, then, means much more than making love or feeling sexually attracted to another person.

Chapter 3—Premarital Sex

Here are some reasons why young people have premarital sex:

- **It's a progression**—Holding hands leads to hugging, to kissing, to French kissing, to petting, and finally to sexual intercourse. You want a little more each time because sexual desire grows. When you begin holding hands, you won't go back to not holding hands. When you end your date with a kiss, soon you will greet each other with a kiss and say good-bye with several.
- **Began dating early**—The younger kids are when they begin to date, the more likely they are to have sex before graduating from high school. 2

Age dating begins	Percent who have sex before graduation
▪ 12 yrs	91 percent

- 13 yrs   56 percent
- 14 yrs   53 percent
- 15 yrs   40 percent
- 16 yrs   20 percent

  o "The percentage of high school students who have had sexual intercourse increases by grade. In 2003, 62 percent of twelfth graders had had sexual intercourse, compared with 33 percent of ninth graders." 3

  o "The younger a girl is when she has sex for the first time, the greater the average age difference is likely to be between her and her partner." 4

- **It's a great feeling**—Emotions are created and given to us by God, but they are not meant to determine our decisions and set the boundaries of our values. (Having sex can also be painful and unpleasant for the girl, and afterward both can feel guilt, hurt, pain, and regret.)

- **Lack of knowledge about sex**—Friends and even a health class at school may teach some basic anatomy and the basics of using protection, but they won't teach the sanctity of sex. (They rarely ever teach you that having sex can ruin your life.) The church should be involved in educating its young people about God's way.

- **A broken home**—With few adult role models these days, young people lose sight of right and wrong. Influence and pressure from friends becomes stronger than that in the home, so the closeness and sharing that should take place in the family is sought elsewhere. Lack of security in the home may cause a young person to look for intimacy with other people.

- **Fear of being alone**—Some young people are embarrassed or afraid of being alone. They try to buy security by "giving sex." What they really want is a steady relationship, not sex.

- **Rebellion**—Some kids choose a lifestyle based on what Mom and Dad don't want, either to hurt their parents or to get attention. (You will hurt more after you have sex than you will if you just get mad at your parents. Think of the consequences to you before you go and do something stupid like that.)

- **Peer pressure**—Some kids fall into the trap of doing what friends pressure them to do for the sake of popularity or reputation. Friends tell you that if you don't do it then you are not cool.

Why does God say to wait until marriage?

- **It's a sin against your body**—"... abstain from fornication; that every one of you should know how to possess his vessel in sanctification and honor"

(I Thessalonians 4:3–4). "… he who sins sexually sins against his own body" (I Corinthians 6:18). Also see I Corinthians 6:15–20.

- **It affects your walk with God**—Your relationship with God will be damaged. When you begin to go down in your spiritual life, you will be more apt to fall into other types of ungodly behavior. When having sex becomes more important to you than what God says, priorities in general will change.

- **It affects your influence on others**—The Bible says that you should not cause other Christians to stumble in their walk with the Lord. (See Romans 14:21.) What kind of example are you being to non-Christians?

- **You can get hurt**—The chances of getting hurt are high. Everything has a price, and sex without real commitment is no exception. "Not many teenage girls accept sex for the sake of sex; she thinks, 'I love.' He feels trapped and stops calling. Her world shatters. Picking up the pieces isn't easy. Afterward, other guys figure her for an easy mark. It's not a hard decision to make when a teen asks, 'Will I like myself if I make this choice?' A little selfishness helps. 'Whom will I hurt? Will it be myself?'" 5

- **It's not a test of love**— "If you really love me, prove it," is a phrase used since the beginning of time. On the contrary, guys are less likely to take advantage of a girl they love and admire and are more likely to care about her feelings, desires, and welfare.   He will not try to talk her into something she has not asked for. Anyone who says sex is proof of love is not saying "I love you," but rather "I love *it*." Sex does not grow into love, but rather love must grow into sex.

- **It doesn't prepare you for marriage**—Preparing with proper sex education, not premarital sex, will remove the fear of the unknown. The argument that "practice makes perfect" is not true with sex. Premarital sex is a casual affair that often happens in conditions that are less than ideal. Fear of getting caught and having guilt are usually present. "On the other hand, sexual relationships in marriage are a mutual sharing of oneself with your lover. The chief interest is not yours but your lover's satisfaction. To be a real sexual expert in marriage, you must know the needs and idiosyncrasies of your partner and respond to him or her as a person. Such knowledge or experience does not come from having sexual relationships with many partners before marriage, but comes from loving and living with a person. No amount of technical expertise makes one a good husband or wife." 6   Why not learn together on your wedding night with your own spouse? How would you feel about someone practicing with your wife or husband or sister or brother?

- **God has an order concerning marriage**—In Matthew 19:3, Jesus shows that marriage involves:

a. Leaving	a. "For this reason a man shall leave his father and mother"
b. Cleaving	b. "and be joined to his wife"
c. Becoming one (sexual intercourse)	c. "and the two shall become one flesh."

The "one flesh" relationship (sexual intercourse) follows the leaving and the cleaving. It does not precede it. There is no such thing as a "trial marriage." You can't call living together before marriage a real test. If you can't commit to each other legally (by getting married) when your relationship is good and happy, then how do you expect those traits to stay with you when times get tough? The word "commit" means to bind as by a promise; to pledge. That is God's way for marriage.

- **The Bible warns against fornication**—see definitions.

- **To maintain order and harmony**—Our society is built on rules. Unmarried sex breaks them down. Rules are necessary in every area of life to keep order and harmony. Physically, we must eat food and drink water or we will die. In sports, if everyone did his or her own thing there could be no game. In society, we have laws against stealing from, murdering, or hurting others. Every area of life has rules. We must see the rules as helping us, not hurting us. Saving sex for marriage is God's way of having order and harmony in your life so you can have the fulfilled life God planned for you.

- **To close other doors**—Dishonesty, greed, selfishness, war, cruelty, dirty politics, hypocrisy, willfully hurting or using your friends—these are wrong, whereas shared love seems so right. "But sex outside of marriage hardly ever lasts long before some of the wrongs creep in; for when you break one rule, others are weakened. This is especially true in teen love affairs, in which secrecy produces guilt, and uncertainty makes partners over-possessive. Guilt then moves to depression." 7

- **It hinders communication**—The greatest emotional drive is not for sex, but for a closeness that will cure loneliness. Sex becomes the main focus of their relationship. "All week long I find myself just living for the weekend when we can hop into bed together." "We're finding that our whole relationship centers more and more around sex these days." "Since we've begun having regular sex relations, we're finding that our communication in other areas is breaking down." "When we're together, we don't talk much anymore; we take for granted that our time together will be spent engaging in sex. Somehow, though, I feel we're missing something—that we're not relating to each other as persons lately, just bodies." 8

- **You are not ready**—The urge to have a baby is especially strong in women, but a teen affair is not a good time. As a nation, we have available to anyone the means to prevent pregnancy, but the United States still has the highest teen pregnancy rate of any industrialized country. About 40 percent of American women become pregnant before the age of twenty. Unless you are ready to be a mom or dad for the next eighteen years, you need to stay away from sex.

- **Somebody pays**—Babies pay for their parents' "free sex" sometimes by dying as a result of abortion. Sometimes they pay with birth defects caused by sexually transmitted diseases. No sexual encounter is free if others have to pay for it. Sow obedience to the rules of God, and you will reap benefits. Sow disobedience to the rules of God, and you will reap consequences.

- **Virginity is desirable**—If you catch a guy or girl alone they will most often tell you that virginity does make one more desirable. It is his/her desire to be the first and the last with you. Here's a comment from a teenage guy: "When you're involved physically, the line gets blurred between love and hormones. From then on, you're always wondering which factor is in play. Do

I like this girl, or do I just like the physical pleasure? And that confusion totally messes things up." 9

- **It can affect your future**—An intense love affair can mean the end of college plans or a professional career.

- **Anyone can have sex**—If the man and woman are physically normal, they are capable of intercourse, but fulfilled sex is a process, not a sudden event. It is something that normally improves steadily as you grow together as a couple. Healthy sex comes more from communication than technique. Intimacy is not sex. A prostitute can have sex, but her relationships are not intimate at all.

- **Waiting builds trust**—"If you had sex with me how do I know you won't do it again. If someone better comes along will you leave me?" Waiting builds self-control, which demonstrates trust to your partner. The more you can trust someone, the more comfortable you will feel sharing emotionally. When you can control yourself sexually, you can control yourself in other areas.

- **To protect you from guilt**—Guilt is a result of premarital sex that may haunt you more than any other. Every time you see that person or pass the place, you will have memories of those previous times. It is like trying to unscramble eggs. You can't do it.

Additional Thoughts

- What you do with your emotions and your body is too important to be decided by others. Here is a place where you need to think for yourself.

- You should never be in bondage to sex. Young people caught up in their own passion having sex are slaves to sex. When sex is the master, it can destroy relationships and even the joy that sexual excitement should bring. That is why God tells us to control our sexual drives. Couples who desire a godly relationship need to set aside the sexual part and develop their hearts and spiritual selves.

- Christianity is measured in terms of what we do—not in terms of what we don't do. The Christian says "no" to sex as a plaything, in order to say "yes" to sex as an expression of love. God's way is the most romantic and beautiful way.

- A girl offers sex because what she wants is love. A guy offers love because what he wants is sex.

- Many people agree that our American youth are threatened by alcohol, drugs, cigarette smoking, and violence, but few speak out about the risk to youth from sex outside of marriage. They will mention teen pregnancy and abortion but overlook premarital sex.

About 50 percent of American youth have premarital sex before graduating from high school.

- Young people today are maturing sexually at an earlier age. This means that kids today face a much longer interval between sexual maturity and marriage than their grandparents did. In 1870, the average age of puberty was sixteen years old. Today, by twelve years old, most girls are having their period. In 1870, the average marriage age was eighteen years old. Today many are in their twenties and thirties. That means the average interval between puberty and marriage back in the 1800s was about two years. Today the average interval is between ten and twenty years. So, put together earlier sexual maturation and later marriages, then combine that with all of the media sexual pressure, and top it off with the breakdown of the American family, and it is not surprising to see why teens today are so sexually active. Kids today are also more intellectually prepared for sex than any other generation, but, sadly, not emotionally prepared.

- "63 percent of teens who use alcohol and 70 percent of teens who are frequent drinkers have had sex compared to 26 percent of those who never drank." 10

- Most guys are attracted to girls that have both inner and outer beauty. They might notice the outer beauty first, but it is the sweet, approachable inner beauty that captivates and holds them. The Bible speaks of having a gentle and quiet spirit. (I Peter 3:4)

• What really attracts a girl to a guy is his personality. She looks for someone who is thoughtful, sensitive, and will talk to her.

Chapter 4—What Can You Do to Stay Pure?

Go slow when it comes to the physical part of your relationship. When you like someone, any physical contact is sexually arousing to some degree. Don't go past light kissing. There is a reason for this. Long, deep kissing and the touching of each others genitals are a normal part of the sex act in marriage. It is called foreplay, and it is a natural way to prepare the mind and body for sex. If you don't want to go all the way, then you will not want to do any foreplay.

Men are very easily and quickly aroused. Just a look or a thought is enough for a guy to get intensely excited. That is why girls should watch how they dress in order to make it easier on the guy. The female is not aroused nearly as fast as the guy. Hers is more a feeling of being loved, a feeling of security and emotional bonding. A girl is also aroused by touch, so, guys, you can help her by not touching her in certain areas. I Corinthians 7:1 says, "It is good for a man not to touch a woman."

Begin your relationship by showing your date that you are special. There are some jokes you don't laugh at, some places you won't go, some things you won't do. Show your date that you possess:

Self-respect:
God loves you and made you special. Show your date that you expect to be treated with respect, and you will be. They will have as much respect for you as you have for yourself. Anyone who tries to pressure you into anything you feel is wrong is not worthy of you. No girl who respects herself will let a boy paw her.

Self-confidence:
Have confidence in yourself. Thoughts like, "But I might lose him/her" will be your downfall. If you lose that person, you'll be better off. Wait for someone who has the same standards you do. The type of person you date will determine the type of husband/wife you have, and that will determine your lifestyle. Don't settle for less than what you want.

Set standards ahead of time. Make a list of definite rules that you won't break: "I will not do …" or "I will not go to …" Don't be afraid to share your standards with your date when you begin a relationship. This will keep everything right out front from the beginning. Avoid certain places and parties that might tempt you to compromise. Teens who love God will not go to a Friday-night party where they know there will be drugs and alcohol.

Two Christians on a date must share the responsibility for the actions on that date. It should never be up to the girl alone or up to the guy alone. God holds both accountable. Don't let premarital sex even be an option! To stay pure, spend more time in activities together with other couples or other friends. This decision is a heart purity. There are many ways of saying "no"—"Let's watch TV" or "Let's take a walk" are good ways to say no. Anyone who tries to push you beyond your standards does not really care for you as a person and is selfish.

Be accountable to someone about your dates. You will be more careful if you know you will have to tell someone what you did.

You must learn to control your thought life. The battle is won or lost in your mind. There are steps to getting control of your mind:

1. Confess all evil thinking as sin—I John 1:9
2. Walk in the Spirit—Galatians 5:16–25
3. Ask God for victory—I John 5:14–15
4. Avoid all suggestive material (movies, TV, pornography)—"As a man thinks in his heart so is he"

(Proverbs 23:7). "The eye is the lamp of the body" (Matthew 6:22) (gateway to your mind).

5. Realize that the thought may come to your mind, but you don't have to let it stay there. Force yourself to think on different things (II Corinthians 10:5).

6. Know you are in a spiritual warfare—John 10:10. The devil wants to steal, kill, and destroy you.

Suggestions for young people:

1. Avoid wrong friends. If you run with a sexually active crowd, you will be tempted to be like them. The Bible says in II Corinthians 6:17, "Wherefore come out from among them, and be ye separate saith the Lord."

2. Avoid looking again. Sometimes you can't help the first look, but you can stop looking again.

3. Control the conversation. Don't speak, or listen to, the dirty joke or the off-color story. "Evil communications corrupt good manners" (I Corinthians 15:33).

4. Be careful what you read and watch. Much sex is portrayed in reading material and, of course, TV, movies, and the Internet.

5. Guard your leisure time. Be careful where you go and even what you think about.

6. Have prayer with your date before each time you go out. Jesus will help you to stay pure.

7. Spend time reading the Bible. In Psalms it says, "Thy word have I hid in mine heart, that I might not sin against thee." The more of the Bible you know, the more you will recognize sin immediately and the stronger you will be to say no to it. If you willingly ignore God's word about sex before marriage, you will harden your conscience, not only in this area but in all areas.

8. Have Jesus Christ first in your heart and life. Strong faith in God can keep you pure. Joseph had this faith, and he refused to give in to Potiphar's wife when she came to him and wanted to have sex with him. (Genesis 39:7–20)

9. Instead of focusing on dating and marriage, focus on putting God first and becoming friends with those of the opposite sex. (Matthew 6:33)

10. Get involved in a local church and make friends. (Acts 2:42)

11. Do not be unequally yoked with an unbeliever. This applies to dating, not just to marriage. (II Corinthians 6:14)

Past Mistakes

Maybe some of you have already had sexual intercourse. You're not doomed. God offers lots of love and lots of forgiveness. Read about some in the Bible:

Luke 7:50—The prostitute wept at Jesus' feet.

John 4:6–18—The woman at the well had five husbands and was presently living with another man.

John 8:1–11—This is the story of an adulterous woman.

Hosea—God told Hosea to take back his prostitute wife and forgive her.

II Samuel 11:2–12, 24—This shows the adultery of David and Bathsheba.

Christ offers us his forgiveness and a new start, then it is up to us to live right from then on. Joel 2:25 says, "I will restore the years the locust have eaten." If you want God to restore, then you may have to give up the locust (boyfriend/girlfriend).

If you have blown it, here are several important steps to take:

1. Admit your sin (I John 1:9)
2. Accept God's forgiveness (I John 1:9)
3. Show you are sorry by not doing it again
4. Forgive yourself
5. Don't let Satan deceive you (Romans 8:1)
6. Realize you are a new creation now (II Corinthians 5:17)

Chapter 5—All about Love

Love is a word we throw around a lot today. We say, "I love my dog," "I love pizza," "I love football," "I love my boyfriend/girlfriend." We use the same word, but there are lots of different meanings for the verb *to love*. The Greeks had several words for love.

Eros is the Greek word for physical, sexual love. This is not a deep meaningful love, but it is based on sexual attractiveness only. This is the love that is blind. Under the influence of eros, you will think that you have *phileo, storge*, and *agape* love. Sadly, some people never get past eros love and base their relationship purely on sexual attraction. This is a good reason to postpone physical intimacy that results in eros until after the other "loves" have been developed and tested and you are married.

Phileo is the Greek word for brotherly love. This does not mean brotherly in the sense of family, but in friendship. This is the love that makes you want to help others. Do you enjoy working together, talking about important things together, discussing spiritual things, praying together, and playing together? Do you have common interests?

Storge is the love between family members. It is the love of a mother, father, brother, and sister. This is a strong type of love and involves commitment.

Agape is the Greek word for the God-like love. It is the highest form of love there is. This is an unconditional love for others in spite of their flaws and weaknesses. This love helps us to love others when they are being unlovely. This love desires the best for the one loved. It has nothing to do with emotions. I Corinthians 13:4–7 tells us what is involved in agape love. ("Love is patient, love is kind. It does not envy, it does not boast, it is not proud. It is not rude, it is not self-seeking, it is not easily angered, it keeps no record of wrongs. Love does not delight in evil but rejoices with the truth. It always protects, always trusts, always hopes, always perseveres."). This love needs to be cultivated for it to grow. You can only get this type of love if you put the needs of others a priority in your life.

When you have true love that is ready for marriage, it should involve all of the kinds of love. Eros is wonderful, but it alone is not enough to hold two people together in the everyday stresses of life. Lovers need to be more than lovers; they also need to be best friends—that is have phileo. You don't have to be around someone very long before you see things about them that are unlovely or displeasing to you. At that point, you need agape love to keep the relationship going.

Jesus was always showing agape and phileo love in everything He did. He had compassion for people and healed them (Mark 1:41; Luke 7:13). He accepted sinners (Luke 15:11 and 18:10). He was a friend of tax collectors and outcasts (Luke 7:34).

Chapter 6—Is It Love or Infatuation?

Infatuation is an emotion that can change when circumstances change. Love is a commitment to the other person even when you don't feel any emotions.

Infatuation happens very quickly. It starts with feelings of attraction. With time, the feelings fade. Love goes in the opposite direction. Love usually starts slowly and grows with time.

Infatuation is accompanied by a sense of uncertainty. You want to trust but you are suspicious. When you are apart, you wonder if he/she is with another person. Sometimes you even check to make sure. Jealousy does not come from love. Love begins with a feeling of security. Love means to trust. You want the other person near; but, if not, you know he/she is yours.

Infatuation can be very possessive. "Let's get married right away. I can't chance losing him/her." Love says, "We don't have to rush into anything. We are sure of one another." Love gives freedom to have other friends and other interests.

Infatuation naturally has sexual excitement. You enjoy each other because you know the enjoyment will end in sex. Infatuation runs by passion. Love runs by respect. Love enjoys just being with the other person.

Infatuation can happen again soon after a prior relationship has ended. Love may slowly develop again.

With infatuation, boredom is frequent and partners rely on doing things to have a good time. With love, you find joy in your common interests and just in each other.

Infatuation may "use" the other person. How do you feel several hours after having sex? Do you feel regret? Infatuation takes; love gives. Love is protective of the other and truly cares for him or her.

Infatuation dissolves when problems come. Imagine the person you are dating forty years from now when they are overweight. Would that change how you feel about them? Love overcomes problems that arise. Love accepts unconditionally.

Infatuation wears blinders to block out the faults of one and thinks everything will be okay. Love knows all the faults of the other and loves him or her anyway.

Infatuation might lead you to do things that you might be sorry for, but love never will. Love lifts you up. It is a conscious choice to commit. It makes you a better person than you were before.

How Do You Know What Love Is?

That is hard to answer because love is not a specific thing. It is the total feeling you have about another person. Many times you feel love, infatuation, and even lust all at the same time. To be sure that this feeling is really mature love, you have to know:

- Has it grown with the passing of time?
- Has it brought out the best in you?
- Have you faced problems together and overcome them? Does it carry you through an argument or do you get depressed?
- Have you been yourself, or do you have to live up to someone else's false image?
- Is your love kind, tender, thoughtful, forgiving? (These are the qualities suggested in I Corinthians 13.)
- Spend time apart and see how you feel. Do you miss him or her, or do you find yourself attracted to others?
- Why were you attracted to the person? Is it because of his or her good looks, dynamic personality, way of dressing? *Or* does that person have deep inner qualities such as honesty, meekness, kindness, and a love for God?

- What is your attitude of love?
  - "I'll love you if …"
  - " I love you because …" (These are examples of conditional love.)
  - "I love you"—This love thinks of the other person first. This person gives without taking. This is real love; the first two aren't.
  - Do you respect and trust each other? Are you allowed the private time and space you need to develop as an individual? Can you share your deepest thoughts and know that they will be respected and kept confidential?
  - Do you give more than you get and not keep score? Does your love bring a strong desire in each to make the other person happy?

How do you know if you are in love? Actions speak louder than words. Love goes past good times and sticks with you in bad times too.

Chapter 7—Dating

The most important decision you will make in your life is your decision to accept Jesus as your Lord and Savior. The second most important decision you make is choosing whom you will marry. This will pretty much determine your happiness in life. Because of that, dating is vitally important.

Put growing spiritually first, before finding a mate. Focus on God and what He wants for your life. He will help you make the best decisions in your dating life. Involve yourself in ministry so you can develop character and learn to work with others. All that will help you in your dating and marriage.

The guy should be the spiritual leader. God set it up that way for a reason. The guy is the protector both physically and spiritually. It should be that the closer the girl gets to her guy, the closer she gets to God. Never date an unbeliever because you think you can witness to them. He or she might go to church with you, not because of a desire to learn about God, but because of a desire to spend time with you. More times than not, a nonbeliever will pull you down spiritually. The minute you decide to date a non-Christian, you are saying that you don't want God's will for your life. Your date should not only be a Christian, but he or she should have the same calling on his or her life as you do. If you feel called to be a missionary, then only marry someone else who has that same calling. If you feel called to be in full-time ministry, then only marry someone who can live with that calling.

Respect your parents' judgment when it comes to your date. How does your date act around your family and friends? Be open to their input. They can see things you might not because of your emotions for that person.

Only date someone whom you could see yourself marrying. Dating can, and should, help you find out what kind of personality you need in a mate. Do you like someone who is quiet or someone who is more outgoing? Does he or she have a lot of the same interests you do? Do you both agree on the major issues that will affect a marriage such as which church you will go to, how many times a week you will attend church, what things you spend money on, where you will spend holidays, how you will raise your children? Most importantly, you should agree on the doctrines of the Bible.

Does he or she respect you and your ideas and opinions? Is he or she open to hear your input on something? Does he value your opinion and not just expect you to submit to whatever he decides because he's the guy? How is your communication with each other? Can you talk openly and honestly with good communication skills? Can you be angry with each other and solve problems in a godly way? Have you seen the other person angry with other people? How does he or she react?

How does he or she treat his or her parents? How a person talks to his or her parents and treats them is how he or she will eventually talk to and treat you. What is his or her home life like? How do his or her parents talk to each other? That is what your date is used to, and, many times, all he or she knows, so that is how he or she will talk and act. How does he or she treat other people?

Are his or her work ethics the same as yours? Is he willing to be the main provider? Do you agree on whether the wife should work outside the home or be a stay-at-home mom? (This decision may have to be made in the future, but it is very important to know the answer early on in the relationship.)

After going out with this person, did you feel pressure to have sex? Thinking that if you don't date this person now you may never get another chance is the wrong reason for going out with someone.

Chapter 8—How Far Is Too Far?

Over the years of working with youth, the same question always comes up. "How far is too far in a relationship?" The Bible doesn't really talk about holding hands, kissing, hugging, or petting. Back in my day, "petting" was the term used for touching the breasts and genitals. Let's take a look at this.

First, I believe your idea shouldn't be to see how far you can go without getting into trouble, but how pure you can stay. Make it your business to be spiritually responsible for your actions.

Second, remember that the person you are dating has feelings and emotions, and what you do will either uplift or cause damage to him or her later. That guy or girl is precious not only to God, but to his or her family and friends.

Sexual arousal usually begins so slowly that you might not realize it's happening. Because it is progressive, one thing just naturally leads to another. The progression is usually like this: Holding hands, hugging, lightly kissing, intense kissing, petting, and intercourse. If you don't want to go too far, then you should stop with the light kissing. Anything past that will arouse an intense desire that will lead to sex. You need to make the decision before you go out on your date. Set your mind ahead of time on where you will draw the line. Don't wait until you are too heated to make that decision. Don't go to places where you can be alone and be tempted. Think ahead. Plan ahead to stay pure.

Chapter 9—Sexually Transmitted Diseases

One of the most destructive and permanent results of premarital sex is acquiring a sexually transmitted disease (STD). People are paying the price for sex outside of marriage. Sexually transmitted diseases are no longer reserved for prostitutes or wayward GIs in foreign countries. These diseases are very common in the United States today. Of course, the more sex partners a person has, the greater their chance of getting a STD. There used to be a handful of sexually transmitted diseases, now there are dozens. I will outline a few of the major ones.

AIDS

What are HIV and AIDS?

Human immunodeficiency virus (HIV) is a virus that destroys the immune system. HIV targets the cells in your blood that help the body fight disease. Over many years, the cells will be destroyed, then the body will have a weaker defense against infection. Some forms of cancer may also occur. When infections and other problems occur as a result of the loss of cells, then the person is said to have AIDS (Acquired Immune Deficiency Syndrome). In plain words, HIV is being infected with a virus, and AIDS is when it has turned into a disease. Since AIDS was first reported in the United States in 1981, the number of new victims has doubled each year.

How does a person become infected with HIV?

You cannot get HIV from hugging, kissing, holding hands, sitting on toilet seats, or sharing clothes. More than half of the women who have HIV got it from a sexual partner. It is spread from blood, semen, or other body fluids (except saliva) from a person who already has HIV. This can happen through sex, a blood transfusion, or sharing a needle with an infected person. Today, blood donations are tested before they are used.

Who is at risk for HIV infection?

The HIV infection is more common today than it was in years past. In general, homosexuals or any one having multiple partners are at greater risk of HIV infection. Even if you have only been with one partner, but that partner has had several partners, you are at a greater risk. "Since most people who are infected with HIV appear healthy, a blood test for the virus is necessary to see who has the infection. People who have a positive blood test for HIV are called HIV-positive." There are more heterosexuals infected today than there were homosexuals infected five years ago. The difference between men with HIV and women with HIV is that women often have additional problems such as repeated vaginal yeast infections, especially as the immune system becomes weaker. Also, more serious infections such as pelvic disease and cancer can be harder to treat if a woman has HIV.

Is there a treatment for AIDS?

"There are prescription medicines that are an option, but they do not cure the HIV infection or AIDS, and do not prevent passing HIV to others." 11

Chlamydia

Chlamydia (pronounced "cla-MI-dee-ah") is a bacterium (germ) that both men and women catch through sexual contact with someone who is infected.

How common is Chlamydia?

Chlamydia is the most frequently reported bacterial sexually transmitted disease in the United States. It probably is under reported because most people with Chlamydia are not aware they have it.

How do people get this infection?

"Chlamydia can be transmitted during vaginal, anal, or oral sex. The greater the number of sex partners, the greater the risk of infection." You are at risk if you have had sex with a new partner, have had many sex partners, or have had a partner who has had many sex partners. Because the cervix (opening to the uterus) of teenage girls and young women is not fully matured and is probably more susceptible to infection, these are the women who are at particularly high risk for this infection if they are sexually active.

What are the symptoms of Chlamydia?

Chlamydia is known as a "silent" disease because about three-quarters of infected women and about half of infected men have no symptoms. When symptoms do occur, they can include:

- Painful urination (a burning sensation)
- Vaginal discharge in women
- Pain during sexual intercourse
- Pain in the lower abdomen
- Irregular periods in women
- A discharge from the penis in men
- Trouble getting pregnant

- Pain in the testicles in men
- "Men or women who have receptive anal intercourse may acquire a chlamydial infection in the rectum, which can cause rectal pain, discharge, or bleeding. Chlamydia can also be found in the throats of women and men who have had oral sex with an infected partner." 12

Gonorrhea

"Gonorrhea is caused by *Neisseria gonorrhoeae*, a bacterium that can grow and multiply easily in the warm, moist areas of the reproductive tract, including the cervix (opening to the womb), uterus (womb), and fallopian tubes (egg canals) in women, and in the urethra (urine canal) in both women and men. The bacterium can also grow in the mouth, throat, eyes, and anus."

How common is Gonorrhea?

Gonorrhea is so common that The Centers for Disease Control (CDC), estimates that more than 700,000 people in the United States get the infection every year. Only about half of these infections are reported to the CDC.

How do people get Gonorrhea?

"Gonorrhea is spread through contact with the penis, vagina, mouth, or anus. Ejaculation does not have to occur for gonorrhea to be transmitted or acquired."

Anyone who has received treatment may get infected again if they are sexually active with another person who has gonorrhea.

What are the symptoms of Gonorrhea?

Some men with gonorrhea may have no symptoms at all. Other men can have symptoms anytime from two to five days after infection—or it could take as long as thirty days. Symptoms and signs include a burning sensation when urinating, or a white, yellow, or green discharge from the penis. Sometimes men with gonorrhea get painful or swollen testicles. In women, the symptoms of gonorrhea are often mild, but most women who are infected have no symptoms. Even when a woman has symptoms, they can be so non-specific as to be mistaken for a bladder or vaginal infection. The initial symptoms and signs in women include a painful or burning sensation when urinating, increased vaginal discharge, or vaginal bleeding between periods. Women with gonorrhea are at risk of developing serious complications from the infection. "Symptoms of rectal infection in both men and women may include discharge, anal itching, soreness, bleeding, or painful bowel movements." Rectal infection also may cause no symptoms. Infections in the throat may cause a sore throat but usually cause no other symptoms.

If not treated, gonorrhea can cause serious and permanent health problems in both women and men. In women, gonorrhea is a common cause of pelvic inflammatory disease (PID). In men, gonorrhea can cause epididymitis, a painful condition of the ducts attached to the testicles that may lead to infertility if left untreated.

Is there treatment for gonorrhea?

Several antibiotics can be prescribed for gonorrhea, but successful treatment is becoming more difficult. "Because many people with gonorrhea also have chlamydia, another STD, antibiotics for both infections are usually given together. Persons with gonorrhea should be tested for other STDs. Although medication will stop the infection, it will not repair any permanent damage done by the disease. People who have had gonorrhea and have been treated can get the disease again if they have sexual contact with persons infected with gonorrhea." 13

Genital Herpes

Genital herpes (pronounced "HER-pees") is a contagious sexually transmitted disease caused by the herpes simplex virus (HSV). There are many types of HSV.

How do people get genital herpes?

Anyone who is sexually active can get genital herpes. You can get genital herpes if you have sex with an infected person. "Herpes is spread from skin-to-skin contact. It can be spread from one part of the body to another, such as from the genitals to the fingers, to the eyes, or other parts of the body."

What are the symptoms of genital herpes?

Most people infected with HSV are not aware of their infection. However, some people experience flu-like symptoms such as body aches, fever, and headache. Most people who have herpes infection also have outbreaks of sores from time to time. Some individuals with HSV infection never have sores, or they have very mild signs that they do not even notice or that they mistake for insect bites or another skin condition. Other symptoms of genital herpes may include:

- Painful sores in the genital area
- Sore lymph nodes in the groin area
- Vaginal discharge in women
- Painful urination
- Itching

How is genital herpes treated?

"There is no cure for genital herpes. Once you are infected, the virus remains in the body for the rest of your life even if you never experience another outbreak. Your doctor can give you medicine to prevent outbreaks or to help the outbreaks clear up more quickly." 14

Trichomoniasis

Trichomoniasis, (often referred to as "trich"), is a common sexually transmitted disease that affects both women and men, although symptoms are more common in women. Trichomoniasis is caused by a single-celled protozoan parasite.

How do people get trichomoniasis?

The parasite is usually sexually transmitted through penis-to-vagina intercourse or vulva-to-vulva (the genital area outside the vagina) contact with an infected partner. Women can acquire the disease from infected men or women, but men usually contract it only from infected women.

What are the symptoms?

Symptoms of trich can appear anytime between four and twenty-eight days after sex with an infected partner. Sometimes symptoms don't appear at all. In females, symptoms can include:

- abundant and/or frothy vaginal discharge ranging in color from gray to green to yellow, with a watery to milky consistency
- foul odor
- itching and tenderness in or around the vagina
- pain during sex
- bleeding after sex

- pain during urination
- soreness or itching of the genital area

How is trichomoniasis treated?

"Trich can be treated with prescription medications. Both sexual partners should be considered infected and treated at the same time, even if one has no symptoms." 15

Human Papillomavirus

Human papillomavirus (also called HPV) is the most common sexually transmitted disease in the United States. There are more than forty HPV types, but most people who become infected with HPV do not even know they have it.

How do people get HPV?

HPV is normally transmitted through sexual contact. This includes having oral, vaginal, or anal sex with someone who has HPV. "A person who has HPV may not show any signs of the virus, as genital warts often take years to develop. In women, the warts may be on the cervix and therefore not visible." You are more likely to get HPV if you have multiple partners or if your partner has had multiple partners. You are also more at risk if you smoke or you are a woman who doesn't get regular Pap tests.

What are the symptoms of HPV?

Most people with HPV do not develop symptoms or health problems, but certain types can cause genital warts in men and women. Other HPV types can cause cervical cancer and other less common cancers. HPV types are often referred to as "low-risk" (wart-causing) or "high-risk" (cancer-causing) based on whether they put a person at risk for cancer. In 90 percent of cases, the body's immune system clears the HPV infection naturally within two years. This is true of both high-risk and low-risk types.

Low risk: Genital warts usually appear as small bumps or groups of bumps, usually in the genital area. They can be raised or flat, single or multiple, small or large, and sometimes cauliflower shaped.

High risk: Cervical cancer is cancer in the lower part of the uterus. The uterus is the pear-shaped organ in which a baby grows during pregnancy. The cervix forms the canal that opens into the birth canal, which leads to the outside of the woman's body. Cervical cancer does not have symptoms until it is quite advanced.

Can a woman prevent cervical cancer?

The best way is to wait until marriage to have sex and then be faithful to your spouse. That means having sex with each other and no one else. Getting regular Pap tests helps. There is a vaccine now that helps prevent certain types of HPV that cause cancer. The vaccine works best in females who have never had sex. As of now, the shot works for about five years preventing about 70 percent of cervical cancers. About 30 percent of cancers will not be prevented by the current vaccine.

How is HPV treated?

Currently, there is no cure for HPV, but a healthy immune system usually can fight off HPV naturally. There *are* treatments for the diseases that HPV can cause:

Genital warts must be treated by your doctor. Do not try to treat the warts yourself. The over-the-counter wart medicine is not supposed to be used for genital warts, as they can irritate the skin.

"Cervical cancer can be treated when it is diagnosed early. There are new forms of surgery, radiation therapy, and chemotherapy available for patients. Women who get routine Pap testing and follow up as needed can identify problems *before* cancer develops." 16

Syphilis

Syphilis (pronounced "SIFF-uh-liss") is a sexually transmitted disease (STD) caused by the bacterium (germ) *Treponema pallidum.*

How do people get syphilis?

"Syphilis is passed from one person to another during sexual contact. You could get syphilis by touching the blood or sores of a person who has syphilis, especially sores on the person's mouth, penis, vagina, or anus (the opening to the rectum)," but it cannot be spread from a toilet seat, doorknob, swimming pool, hot tub, bathtub, clothing, or eating utensils.

What are the symptoms of syphilis?

The primary stage of syphilis is usually marked by the appearance of a single sore that occurs ten days to three months after exposure. In men, the first sign of syphilis may be a sore on the penis. In women, the first sign may be a sore around or inside the vagina. You might not even notice the sore, because syphilis sores do not usually hurt. The sores go away after three to six weeks, but if you don't get treatment, the infection can progress to the secondary stage. The secondary stage begins with a rash. The rash is usually reddish brown and can show up anywhere on the body (even on the palms of the hands and the soles of the feet). The rash appears two to ten weeks after you see the sores. Other signs of syphilis may include fever, swollen lymph glands, body aches, sores in the mouth, and fatigue.

The latent stage produces no symptoms, but the infection is still present in the body. This latent stage can last for years.

When the infection reaches this stage, it can cause problems in the brain and spinal cord. Syphilis may damage the heart and other organs also.

What is the treatment for syphilis?

Syphilis can be treated with penicillin or other medicines if you are allergic to penicillin. For primary-stage syphilis, you only need to get one shot. For secondary-stage syphilis, you will need two shots. If you have an advanced case of syphilis, you may need stronger treatment. "Treatment will kill the syphilis bacteria and prevent further damage, but it will not repair damage already done." 17

Pelvic Inflammatory Disease

Pelvic inflammatory disease (PID) is an infection of the uterus, fallopian tubes, and ovaries. PID can cause permanent damage to the female reproductive organs. If bacteria gets into the fallopian tubes, it can cause an infection that causes scar tissue. The scar tissue can block the movement of eggs into the uterus. If the fallopian tubes are totally blocked by scar tissue, the sperm cannot fertilize the egg and the woman cannot become pregnant.

How does a woman get PID?

The most common way to get PID is by having sex with a person who already has gonorrhea or chlamydia. These diseases are in the semen and other body fluids. During sex, the bacteria can move from a woman's cervix into her reproductive organs. The germs can also infect the anus. Women under twenty-five years old are more likely to get PID because their cervix is not fully matured, putting them at a risk for sexually transmitted disease, which leads to PID. Of course, the more sex partners a woman has, the greater her chance of getting PID. A woman whose partner has had more than one sex partner is at greater risk also.

What are the symptoms of PID?

Because the symptoms can vary from none to severe, many women don't know they have PID. It goes unrecognized by them and their doctor while it is doing serious damage to their reproductive organs. Women who experience symptoms may have:

- A dull pain and tenderness in the lower abdomen
- Vaginal discharge with an unpleasant smell
- Irregular menstrual periods, such as extra long periods, spotting, or cramps throughout the month
- Chills, high fever, nausea, diarrhea, and vomiting
- Pain during sex
- Low back pain
- Painful urination

What is the treatment for PID?

"Usually PID can be cured with antibiotics. This may require hospitalization if the infection is severe. Although the infection can be cured, the damage already done to the reproductive organs will not go away." 18

Hepatitis B

Hepatitis is an inflammation of the liver. It can be a mild illness that lasts a few weeks or a serious illness that lasts a lifetime. Acute hepatitis is usually a first-time episode with symptoms that last less than six weeks. Most people recover with no problems. In chronic hepatitis, the illness lasts six months or longer and the liver is permanently damaged. The time between acute hepatitis and chronic hepatitis can be short or it can be years. There are five types of hepatitis. This book will just cover B and C, which are the more common types.

How does a person get hepatitis B?

Hepatitis B is spread through contact with blood, semen, or another body fluid from a person who has hepatitis B. You can get hepatitis B through sexual contact, sharing needles, drug equipment, or it can be passed from an infected mother to her baby at birth. You cannot get it from hugging or shaking hands with an infected person.

What are the symptoms of acute hepatitis B?

- nausea
- vomiting
- loss of appetite
- abdominal pain
- jaundice (the skin turns yellow)
- weakness
- fatigue
- brown urine (may look like tea)

If you have a mild case of hepatitis, you may not even realize that you have it. It may only cause symptoms similar to the stomach flu.

What are the symptoms of chronic hepatitis B?

Chronic hepatitis can lead to cirrhosis of the liver. When that happens, the liver cells die and the damaged part of the liver stops working. As cirrhosis gets worse and the liver is damaged, the same symptoms of acute hepatitis B may appear.

What is the treatment for hepatitis B?

There are a number of medical treatments available that are successful. You will have to see a specialist who treats chronic liver problems.

"A vaccine is available to prevent hepatitis B. It is given to all infants, older children, adolescents, and health care workers." 19

Hepatitis C

Hepatitis C is usually spread by contact with blood. This can happen from sharing needles while doing drugs, sharing needles used for tattooing or body piercing, sharing razors, getting accidentally stuck with a used needle, or even having received a blood transfusion before 1992, when the routine testing of blood began. Some of these ways of getting hepatitis C are rare but they do occur. Most people don't know when they contracted hepatitis C. The virus stays in their liver and causes chronic liver damage. There is no vaccine for hepatitis C. Hepatitis C can only be spread from direct contact with infected blood. You cannot get it from hugging, kissing, using public toilets, sharing eating utensils. If you have hepatitis C, you cannot donate blood.

Is there a treatment for hepatitis C?

"There are medicines to treat and possibly cure hepatitis C. Your doctor may also have you take the hepatitis A and B vaccine, and avoid alcohol to prevent further liver damage." 20

Chapter 10—God's Word On ...

All scripture in this section is from the New King James Version unless otherwise stated.

Marriage—between a husband and wife

Genesis 2:18, 24—"And the Lord God said, *It is* not good that man should be alone; I will make him a helper comparable to him. Therefore a man shall leave his father and mother and be joined to his wife, and they shall become one flesh."

I Corinthians 7:3–5—"Husbands and wives should be fair with each other about having sex. A wife belongs to her husband instead of to herself, and a husband belongs to his wife instead of to himself. So don't refuse sex to each other, unless you agree not to have sex for a little while, in order to spend time in prayer. Then Satan won't be able to tempt you because of your lack of self-control." (Contemporary English Version)

Proverbs 18:22—"*He who* finds a wife finds a good *thing,* And obtains favor from the Lord."

I Peter 3:1, 7—"Wives, likewise, be submissive to your own husbands, that even if some do not obey the word, they, without a word, may be won by the conduct of their wives, Husbands, likewise, dwell with them with understanding, giving honor to the wife, as to the weaker vessel, and as being heirs together of the grace of life, that your prayers may not be hindered."

Colossians 3:18,19—"Wives, submit to your own husbands, as is fitting in the Lord. Husbands, love your wives and do not be bitter toward them."

Proverbs 5:18–23—talks about marriage relations

Ephesians 5:22–33—talks about the love of husband and wife

Homosexuality—having sexual desire for another of one's own sex

Leviticus 18:22—"It is disgusting for a man to have sex with another man." (Contemporary English Version)

Romans 1:26, 27—"God let them follow their own evil desires. Women no longer wanted to have sex in a natural way, and they did things with each other that were not natural. Men behaved in the same way. They stopped wanting to have sex with women and had strong desires for sex with other men. They did shameful things with each other, and what

has happened to them is punishment for their foolish deeds."
(Contemporary English Version)

Adultery—sexual intercourse between a married person and another, not the spouse

Scriptures forbidding adultery:

Exodus 20:14—"You shall not commit adultery."

Matthew 5:28—"But I say to you that whoever looks at a woman to lust for her has already committed adultery with her in his heart."

Leviticus 18:20—"Moreover you shall not lie carnally with your neighbor's wife, to defile yourself with her. "

Hebrews 13:4—"Marriage *is* honorable among all, and the bed undefiled; but fornicators and adulterers God will judge."

I Corinthians 6:9, 10—"Surely you know that the people who do wrong will not inherit God's kingdom. Do not be fooled. Those who sin sexually, worship idols, take part in adultery, those who are male prostitutes, or men who have sexual relations with other men, those who steal, are greedy, get drunk, lie about others, or rob—these people will not inherit God's kingdom." (New Century Version)

Fornication—sexual intercourse outside of marriage

Scriptures forbidding fornication:

I Corinthians 5:1, 9—"It is actually reported that there is sexual immorality among you, and of a kind that does not occur even among pagans: A man has his father's wife. I have written you in my letter not to associate with sexually immoral people."Ephesians 5:3—"But among you there must not be even a hint of sexual immorality, or of any kind of impurity, or of greed, because these are improper for God's holy people."

I Thessalonians 4:3–8—"It is God's will that you should be sanctified: that you should avoid sexual immorality; that each of you should learn to control his own body in a way that is holy and honorable, not in passionate lust like the heathen, who do not know God; and that in this matter no one should wrong his brother or take advantage of him. The Lord will punish men for all such sins, as we have already told you and warned you. For God did not call us to be impure, but to live a holy life. Therefore, he who rejects this instruction does not reject man but God, who gives you his Holy Spirit."

Proverbs 5:20, 21—"Why be captivated, my son, by an adulteress? Why embrace the bosom of another man's wife?

For a man's ways are in full view of the Lord, and he examines all his paths."

Proverbs 7—The whole chapter talks about an adulteress woman seducing a man.

Abortion—the termination of a pregnancy

Here are scriptures that show a life begins at conception:

Jeremiah 1:5—"Before I formed you in the womb I knew you; before you were born I sanctified you."

Isaiah 44:24—"Thus says the Lord, your Redeemer, And He who formed you from the womb …"

Job 31:15—"Did not He who made me in the womb make them? Did not the same One fashion us in the womb?"

Luke 1:41, 44—"And it happened, when Elizabeth heard the greeting of Mary, that the babe leaped in her womb; and Elizabeth was filled with the Holy Spirit … For indeed, as soon as the voice of your greeting sounded in my ears, the babe leaped in my womb for joy."

Isaiah 49:1—"The Lord has called me from the womb; from the matrix of my mother He has made mention of my name."

Psalm 139:13–16—"For you created my inmost being; you knit me together in my mother's womb. I praise you because I am fearfully and wonderfully made; your works are wonderful, I know that full well. My frame was not hidden from you when I was made in the secret place. When I was woven together in the depths of the earth, your eyes saw my unformed body. All the days ordained for me were written in your book before one of them came to be."

Matthew 18:10—tells us that children are precious

Proverbs 6:16–17—tells us that God hates hands that shed innocent blood.

On January 22, 1973, the United States Supreme Court, in the case of Roe v. Wade, legalized abortion during all nine months of pregnancy. Even though the abortion rate has declined in the years that followed, there are still 3,700 abortions a day in the United States, which adds up to 1.35 million a year. Incase you don't believe a child begins at conception, read about the growth and development just during the first few months.

Week 5: The baby's brain, spinal cord, heart, and other organs begin to form.

Week 6: Baby's heart begins to beat. Basic facial features begin to appear, including an opening for the mouth and passageways that will make up the inner ear. The digestive and respiratory systems begin to form as well.

Week 7: The baby's brain and face begin to develop.

Week 8: The baby's fingers form. Wrists, elbows, and ankles are clearly visible, and baby's eyelids are beginning to form.

Week 9: Movement begins.

Week 10: The baby's head is becoming more round. The neck begins to develop, and the baby's eyelids begin to close to protect his or her eyes. 21

Most abortions occur between seven to ten weeks after conception. *Diary of an Unborn Child* is also the title of a story from the perspective of a developing embryo. The embryo describes her development from the beginning of her life on March 28 until June 10, and ends with the sentence, "Mother, why did you let them stop my life? We could have been so very happy!" 22 I encourage you to google the title and read it.

Reasons for abortions

A study in 1998 revealed that in 1987 and 1988 women reported the following reasons for choosing an abortion:
- 25.5 percent wanted to postpone childbearing
- 21.3 percent could not afford a baby
- 14.1 percent had relationship problems or partners who did not want the pregnancy
- 12.2 percent were too young, so their parent(s) or other(s) objected to pregnancy
- 10.8 percent decided that having a child would disrupt education or job
- 7.9 percent did not want any (more) children

- 3.3 percent aborted because of risk to fetal health
- 2.8 percent aborted because of risk to maternal health
- 2.1 percent provided other reasons 23

If you would like to do more research on abortion, or you are not convinced that abortion is wrong, I suggest you go to Google.com and search "methods of abortion and at what stages of pregnancy are they used." You will be shocked at the graphic pictures.

Chapter 11—FAQs

Following are some of the actual questions asked by members of our youth group.

1. When are two people married in God's sight?

    We believe they are married at the ceremony, not only in the sight of God but the laws of our land. There is something about a public commitment that makes a relationship stronger. If two people can't really commit themselves to each other through marriage, then I doubt if it is real love.

2. Is there a hang-up in the lust of the flesh?

    Yes, partly because of the Hollywood image today. Sex is in many books, movies, and TV shows—also in the way people dress today. Sexual feelings turn into lust when they grow to be so powerful that they become our master rather than our servant.

3. What is your opinion of French kissing?

>   That is up to the couple. If it arouses you, it should not be done.

4. Should kissing be something special or should a person do it just because he or she had a good time?

>   It depends what kind of a kiss you mean. A peck on the mouth or cheek could say thank you, whereas a longer kiss would say I like you—you're special. A kiss should really be something special.

5. Is sex going all the way or does it include such things as kissing and playing with each other?

>   A heavy make-out situation can start a physical drive toward sex. Playing would be petting, which is foreplay to intercourse. Petting can be skin-to-skin contact or touching through clothing. I Corinthians 7:1 says, "It is good for a man not to touch a woman."

6. Is it okay to have sex if you get protection?

>   No, it is still sin in God's eyes, protection or not.

7. Is abortion absolutely wrong in a case of rape?

>   Yes, abortion is wrong. Two wrongs don't make a right. God considers that baby a life. See Exodus 21:22, 23; Psalms 139:13–16; Exodus 23:7. We can pray that God can use you and the baby for His glory. Rape is

one trauma; putting a woman through an abortion is another trauma. The two together would be too much to handle.

8. What do you do when you like a guy who goes with another girl, but he's not sure about that girl and he likes you too? Neither one of you is sure what you or the Lord wants, but you are praying about it together.

> Keep praying. Are they all Christians? If one is not a Christian, drop that one. If all are Christians, remain friends; date both of them, because, if God wills, love will grow.

9. What is petting?

> Petting involves long, deep kissing; mutual touching; and stimulation of the intimate parts of the body, either through the clothing or by direct contact.

10. Is there anything wrong with petting?

> Unless you want to go all the way, you had better stop before petting. All the activities of petting are normal parts of the sex act in marriage. They are a natural way of preparing the body and mind for intercourse, and this foreplay should be limited to marriage. If God considers our *thoughts* as actual adultery (Matthew 5:28), then petting is certainly the same.

11. How far is okay?

> You have gone too far the moment you cannot righteously satisfy the arousal. You should stop with kissing. I Thessalonians 4:3–6 talks about staying away from sexual sins and controlling your body. If a part of the other person's body is different from yours, then don't touch it. If you are seeking to go as far as possible, your motives are wrong.

12. Is it wrong to be a Christian and always be making out?

> There should be a balance in your life. To get to know someone, you need to talk and do things together. Too much making out is bound to lead to other things. Also, it does not look right—what will others think of you?

13. Is it wrong to show your emotions of love for someone in front of other people? Is it wrong to want to have a companion of the opposite sex?

> It is perfectly normal to want a companion of the opposite sex. There is nothing wrong with holding hands, a hug, or a slight kiss in front of others, but not gushy stuff. It embarrasses those around you.

14. How long does sexual intercourse last?

> That's up to the couple. On the sly, probably not too long because of worrying about getting caught.

15. What do you do when you go out and the other person wants to have sex?

> You say "no." If the other person persists, don't go out with him or her anymore.

16. Is it all right for an engaged couple to have sex?

> No, that would still be sex before marriage. Plans don't always end up in reality, and some have had broken engagements.

17. Why does sex have a bad meaning?

> It doesn't really. God created it to be beautiful, but just like any part of God's creation, man has distorted it.

18. Jesus wasn't married was He? What is the right age to marry?

> No, Jesus wasn't married. It does depend upon the couple when it's the right time to get married. At around twelve to fourteen years of age, the body speeds up into growth and development, but the mind doesn't. A boy or girl is physically able to become a father or mother years before he or she is qualified to assume the responsibilities of parenthood. Marriage is really a career. One is not ready to enter any career until one is fully prepared. To be ready for marriage, both the girl and the boy must be able to manage basic life skills. That means they must be able to prepare meals, wash

clothes, manage money, and keep a job, to name a few. Marriage is no place to start learning these skills.

19. If you have had sex before but have asked God to forgive, what do you do when you yourself can't forgive or forget?

We have to stand on the Word of God, not ourselves. I John 1:9 says, "If we confess our sins, he is faithful and just to forgive us our sins." Romans 8:1 says, "There is therefore now no condemnation to them which are in Christ Jesus." Other scriptures are Hebrews 8:12 and Hebrews 10:17. Then Philippians 3:13 says, "… forgetting those things which are behind, and reaching forth unto those things which are before."

20. Does being a Christian mean you can't get emotionally involved with a guy or a girl?

As long as the girl or guy is a Christian, it is perfectly fine to have a boyfriend or girlfriend. It's absolutely normal!

21. Should you discuss previous sexual experiences with your fiancé/fiancee?

Yes, it is best to be honest with each other. You can say "yes" and go no further—no names or details. If that's not good enough, then think again about marrying him or her.

22. If boys get sexually excited, are they committing adultery?

> They have to watch themselves and flee from youthful lust and think on the things of God in order to please God, not themselves. See Philippians 4:8 and II Timothy 2:22.

23. What is the difference between love and lust?

> Love is a strong and deep affection; the desire to satisfy that person, not yourself.

> Lust is wanting to satisfy yourself; it's about the same as infatuation.

24. What about the cost of being popular when you have to lower your morals to be so?

> It is not wrong to be popular with people as long as you are pleasing God and making sure you are putting Him first. See Galatians 1:10.

25. What is God's view of the relationship between husband and wife?

> Genesis 2:18–24—God loved Adam so much that He gave him Eve to be a help meet to him—not to be a dictator, but to be part of a loving, understanding, sharing, and pleasing-each-other relationship.

Ephesians 5:22—says for wives to submit unto their husbands.

Ephesians 5:25—says for husbands to love their wives as Christ also loved the church.

Ephesians 5:28—says for men to love their wives as their own bodies.

26. Is homosexuality wrong?

Yes. In today's society, homosexuality is being accepted, but God never intended man to be with man or woman to be with woman. See Romans 1:19–32 and Leviticus 20:13.

27. Is it okay to date someone if you are just friends and don't think of him or her as a future marriage partner?

If the other person is a Christian, go out and have fun. There's nothing wrong with that at all. But, if the other person does consider you more than a friend, don't go; you might be leading him or her on.

28. How do you know if God wants you to get married?

If you desire to get married, you probably will. Some people have special ministries that they couldn't do if they were married. If that is the case, God satisfies them and they have no desire to marry. Consider, for example, Paul the apostle. He wrote a great deal of the

New Testament and started a great many churches. He may not have been able to do all that if he had been married.

29. Is there a difference between temptation and sin?

Temptation is not sin. Jesus was tempted in every way just as we are—yet he was without sin (see Hebrews 4:15). You can't help what comes into your mind, but you can make a choice to dwell on it or to think on something else. It is not always easy, but it is very possible.

30. What is sexting?

Sexting is sending nude or semi-nude photos or sexual messages to others on their cell phones. Sexting is becoming very popular. Those same pictures can be forwarded to hundreds of other people, either in the name of fun or as revenge after a breakup. The people who receive the pictures can pass them around school or post them on Web sites like MySpace or anywhere else on the Internet, where they will be impossible to delete. Don't give in to the peer pressure without seriously considering what might come of this. In some places, prosecutors are threatening that students caught with sexting pictures "could face jail time and be registered as sex offenders;" some other places are

demanding that offenders attend a rehab program.
24

For more information, go to Google.com and search
"sexting."

Conclusion

My purpose for writing this book is to show you that God offers a "blessed" life for you. He tells us how to live so we can have the happiest and most rewarding life. The Bible says to "love God with all your heart, soul, mind and strength." When you do that, the purity will be there. I have used a lot of scripture from the Bible in this book because that is where you find strength. If we live by the Bible, we will be pure—not because we have to, but because we want to. My desire is that not just young people will read this book, but that parents, teachers, and youth pastors will read it also. I hope that, by reading this book, you have seen how much God does care about your relationships. If you have given your sex and dating life to God, then He will help you in these areas. If you have messed up, please know that God loves you and forgives you. You can start fresh today. If you have never asked Jesus into your heart, now is the time for you to do that. He loves you so much.

Endnotes

1. Wilson W. Grant, *Love and Sex* (Grand Rapids, Michigan, 1974.), p.33

2. *Why True Love Waits* by Josh McDowell and Bob Hostetler p. 73

3. CDC Youth risk behavior surveillance summary- United States, 2003. Morbidity and Mortality Weekly Report, May 2004, 53 (2)

4. Abma JC, Martinez GM, Mosher WD, Dawson BS. Teenagers in the United States; sexual activity, contraceptive use and childrearing, 2002, National Center for Health Statistics. Vital Health Stat. 23 (24), 2004

5. Helen Battell, *"Helping Teens to Handle Today's Sex Freedom,"* Family Circle, (Nov. 1969)

6. Wilson W. Grant, *Love and Sex* (Grand Rapids, Michigan, 1974), p. 31

7. Letha Scanzoni, *Why Wait* (Grand Rapids, Michigan, 1975), p. 115

8. Letha Scanzoni, *Why Wait* (Grand Rapids, Michigan, 1975). p. 113

9. Shaunti Feldhahn and Lisa Rice, *For Young Women Only*, p. 157

10. Joseph A. Califano Jr. The National Center on Addiction and Substance Abuse

11. Familydoctor.org editorial staff

12. http://www.cdc.gov/std/chlamydia/STDFact-Chlamydia.htm

13. Centers for Disease Control and Prevention, Sexually Transmitted Diseases Treatment Guidelines, 2006. MMWR 2006; 55 (No. RR-11). www.cdc.Gov/std/treatment

14. Facts were taken from familydoctor.org

15. Facts were taken from Centers for Disease Control and Prevention and familydoctor.com

16. Facts were taken from Centers for Disease Control and Prevention and familydoctor.com. and U.S. Department of Health and Human Services Office on Women's Health. http://www.womenshealth.gov.

17. Facts were taken from Centers for Disease Control and Prevention and familydoctor.com.

18. Facts were taken from Centers for Disease Control and Prevention and familydoctor.com.

19. Facts were taken from Centers for Disease Control and Prevention and familydoctor.com.

20. Facts were taken from Centers for Disease Control and Prevention and familydoctor.com.

21. www.mayoclinic.com/health/prenatal-care/PR00112

22. Written by Michele DuVal Aiello; copyrighted in 1973

23. Wikipedia.org/wiki/Abortion_in_the_United_States. Reasons for abortions

24. Brent Bozell III. "The Sadness of Sexting"

Notes

Notes

Notes

Notes

Notes

Notes

Notes

Notes

Notes

Notes

Notes

Notes

Notes

Notes

Notes

Breinigsville, PA USA
13 November 2009

227502BV00001B/4/P